Writing Workshop;

A Guide to

Creating a Culture of Useful Feedback

By

Francesca Grossman

To Nancy

Why We Need This

We all know the way it feels to be encased in doubt, surrounded by the ever growing certainty that as writers we have nothing new or interesting to say, that we have exhausted anything anyone else would want to read, that we are, in a phrase: bad at this.

Every writer (not just every new writer – but every single writer ever) feels this way sometimes. Many writers feel this way all the time, which is one of the reasons they become students, in a quest to get better. What a brave and worthwhile endeavor. They toil away alone in a room trying to create something worthy of readers until their wrinkled hands and atrophied bodies come up looking for some kind of help.

And then this is what we do to them:

We put them at a round table of their peers holding only a pencil or a computer as a shield. Their peers are usually other writers who have been also toiling alone, in their own rooms, with their own atrophied bodies and bubbling brains. They are all tired, unsure and terrified. And then, with out preparation or education, we say: *Go.*

Anyone who has ever been in a writing workshop like this knows what can happen next. The room erupts in vague suggestion at best, cruelty at worst. But here's the most important thing about that - aside from it being unkind, very rarely does that type of feedback lead to actual improvement. Almost always a mean spirited or competitive gunfire of feedback leads to something else: fear. It has traumatized some writers enough to make them stop writing entirely.

This is the exact opposite of what feedback should do. Going to a writing workshop – whether in an MFA or in a lovely location off the coast of Maine for a long weekend – should accomplish the same goal.

It should improve the writing.

The goals for everyone in the room should always be: How can we support this writer to become a better writer? How can this piece improve? How can we use the work in front of us to give the writer clues about what's working and what's not working; what makes us stop to catch our breath; and what makes us confused or unsure? What should the writer do more of? What should the writer let go?

This tends to not be the case. Which is why this book seems important.

To be clear, it is not the student writers and workshop participants who are at fault for not being experts on giving feedback. They give feedback they way they were given feedback in high school, college and beyond.

We, as a country, are terrible at this. In large part, we approach teaching writing from a deficit perspective. We say "here's what you are doing wrong," instead of "here's what you are doing right and here's how you might approach the things you are doing wrong in order to get better." This is not across the board, of course. There are some spectacular high school and college writing teachers. The way these teachers give feedback is as an offering: a learning opportunity. They teach *through* the work and support students as they reach their fullest potential.

One of these spectacular teachers is Dr. Nancy Sommers, formally the Director of the Harvard College Expository Writing Program, currently a mentor and teacher in the Harvard Graduate School of Education. It is her research, experience and example that have helped to shape and guide this book. She offers a similar guide for teachers – *Responding to Student Writers* – that has completely revolutionized hundreds of writing teachers' approach to this whole feedback thing.

Feedback is not only a skill but also an entire field of study. Giving feedback is hard. Giving feedback that leads to improvement is really hard, and essential.

Teachers have an obligation to teach their students how to give written and oral feedback to their peers before students ever are asked to do it, and students have an obligation to learn it before they ever step foot into a workshop.

This book is intended to support that learning. It is intended to provide a structure and a lexicon for giving and receiving feedback that leads to improvement.

The following is a step-by-step guide to changing the narrative on writing workshops. It is designed to offer a framework to create a culture of useful feedback and to prepare participants for a positive and helpful discussion. Because if we are not helpful to each other then what the hell are we doing?

You Have To Care

You are not in this writing gig for the money. You are not in it for the fame. For the first many years of a project's conception, things are difficult. At best, writing is a meditation through which we explore what we think and what we wonder. At worst, and most often, it is an exercise in maddening drudgery. Writing is hard. Revising is hard. Usually, we do it alone.

Along comes a writing class – or a writing workshop – a group of other people for whom writing has become both a blessing and a curse. *Fabulous,* you think. These are your people. You can get some help and be around other writers one night a week. There's a cure for the loneliness; there's a cure for the stuck.

You enter the group ready to work deeply on your piece. You are open and eager. You are willing to take some criticism if it serves your own improvement. You are ready to engage and offer feedback to other writers.

That's not enough.

You also have to care.

You have to care about another writer's work almost as much as you care about your own. It seems impossible – you have been working on your particular project for a year and you just read this writer's convoluted draft last night, and it's awful. No, it really is. It's not just your opinion; it is objectively horrendous. You cannot think of one thing that would make this piece palatable. You cannot think of one thing that would make this writer skillful. You cannot think of one thing that will make this piece work.

It doesn't matter. If you don't go into the workshop from a place of empathy, kindness and caring, you might as well not go in at all.

This seems obvious – you should care - true for every interaction in life, but this is not a call to be *nice*; this is a call to *care*. Caring is honest, but never cruel, it is invested and interested. It is authentic and pulls from the very heart of the matter: that this writer is a human and this human deserves our positive attention and support in order to become a better writer.

There are other practical reasons to care:

- Having a consistent writing group, or reader(s) can be an enormous, ongoing support.
- Investing in other writers' work can show you a lot about what works and what doesn't work so that you can apply it to your own writing.
- Giving feedback makes you a better writer. It does. We'll talk about feedback in more depth, but for now it's enough to know that the more you read work in different stages and think about it deeply, the better you'll write.

You Have To Prepare

So we have a basic understanding of how to begin to establish a culture of positive feedback in a writing workshop. You have to care. Now it's time to go deeper into how to prepare for it.

If you aren't planning to read the work and make comments both in the text and at the end of the piece you should skip the workshop. Without a comprehensive set of written feedback as preparation, it is almost impossible to give oral feedback that's useful. Take a walk outside in the sun; that will also do wonderful things for your writing.

Everyone in the writing workshop should be there for the same reason: they want to get better. We can all get better. We should all strive to get better every time we open the computer or take out our pen. The support and feedback we get from a writing workshop should be in service of that goal, and NO OTHER. Writers in a workshop put themselves on the line, risking the pummeling of their deepest ideas and emotions because they have the goal of improvement.

One thing we can all agree does not produce improvement is not writing at all. That seems obvious but think about it. If we give feedback that makes a writer stuck in space, not knowing what to do, or worse, feeling inadequate or inept, and they stop writing as a result, we have failed them. It is – at least in part – our fault. We do not want to fail them. We want them to improve. We all want to improve. In order to improve we must be ready.

So how do you prepare?

Preparing Written Feedback

All Feedback is a Conversation

This conversation starts and ends through the WORK. The middle part of the conversation is where you actually talk to each other in person. Talking to writers happens after you make written comments. What that means is you should never write something on a writer's work that you wouldn't say to them in person. You should treat the work as a conduit into the writer's soul. Heavy, but true. In the workshop, you will have the opportunity to actually talk to the writer directly, but beforehand it's still crucial to remember this is a two-sided conversation – with the goal of improving the work. We are back there again.

Know Where You Are Standing

Where is the writer in the process? Are you reading the first draft or is this something further along? What is the writer looking for? How can you help?

One way to prepare for giving this kind of feedback is for the writer to craft a *Dear Reader* letter. This letter can be attached to the piece at the beginning or end, and asks the fellow workshop participants to focus on specific issues. For example, a line in the letter might be: "I'm not really looking at the language yet, I'm focusing on the structure so any help with that would be great."

If the writer hasn't offered a *Dear Reader* letter, you can ask him for these questions ahead of time. Specific questions get specific answers. It's important to give writers permission to ask for what they need.

There are also different priorities inherent in responding to early drafts and later drafts. It's not useful, for instance, to suggest the sentences are too long in a piece that needs a whole point of view overhaul. Concentrating on a sentence might seem helpful – and might be later on – but in the first drafts the particular sentences become irrelevant. They may all just come out anyway.

There are two important ways to give written feedback on a draft:

Margin Notes

These are, not surprisingly, the notes that live in the margins of the work. They need to be short enough to fit, but long enough to say what you need to say to the writer at that moment. They should, if possible, link to a specific place in the work. If they are general, they should be positive. A "not so good," takes the writer out of the piece. It stings and she wants to know why you didn't tell her more about what was so horrible you stopped to write a note. In contrast, a "lovely," really just reads as "I liked this," and the writer will usually move on. Try to be clear in the margin notes. There is much more detail on this to follow, but if the writer is confused by these notes it will be very hard for her to take the advice to heart.

End Notes – Write a Letter

Especially if the writer wrote you a lovely and helpful *Dear Reader* letter to launch you into the work, do them the courtesy of responding with a letter back. Your endnote can be detailed or more general if the margin notes were comprehensive, but it should summarize how you felt about the piece as a whole and outline one or two larger things you feel the writer could do to improve the draft. It should go right at the end of the piece. It should address the writer directly "Dear Anne," and it should follow in the positive and respectful tone of your other comments

4

The Nitty Gritty of Written Feedback

Read. Then Read It Again

Most likely, the draft you will be responding to will not be polished. Most likely, it will lack clarity and focus. Most likely, you will have to read it a couple of times before you can actually make comments that will improve the work.

So read it at least twice. The first time, do not touch it. Maybe you want to make a few notes to yourself so that you look for specific things when you read it a second time, but do not put pen to paper. Restrain yourself. Just read.

Throw Away The Red Pens

Red pens are cliché and terrifying. They remind us of scary high school English classes and huge "X's" through our work (we'll talk about those in a minute) neither of which puts us in the right frame of mind for giving useful feedback.

Point Out Beauty

This cannot be understated. It is crucial for the work, and for the writer, for you to point out where it's awesome. Say "Yes! Do more of this! This is great," wherever you think it is great and they should do more of it. Pointing out the good will necessarily serve to bypass the not so good. People understand that if you skip some things but say many other things are great, they should spend time beefing up the great and concentrate less on that which you did not mention. Even if you *only* tell a writer what works and don't mention what doesn't, he can improve.

Make Feedback Digestible

People simply can't process too many pieces of information at once, especially about their writing. For that reason, and for your own sanity, it is important to only offer a few large-scale suggestions. If you have a lot of small comments, that's ok, but if you are asking the writer to change the point of view and maybe switch the timeline and therefore you will have to twist the structure around after you add another character who is slightly less relatable than the protagonist, well, you can see what might happen. This kind of inundation is never helpful, and it only serves to show the writer that though you are trying to appear supportive, you are actually saying the piece will only work if she does it your way. Not only is this not true, it's demoralizing and paralyzing. Writers don't know where to start, and often this makes them stop in their tracks.

Look For Patterns

Often, the thing that will be challenging about of piece of writing will happen again and again. This is great news. It's usually difficult to see those patterns in our own work so pointing them out (in a positive tone) can be incredibly helpful. When we identify a pattern, the writer has a map to go back into the work armed with a new framework for revision.

If You Must Use Hieroglyphics They Need Explanation - But Margin Notes Are Better

Make sure *anyone* could understand your notes. If you have symbols you rely on, make a glossary at the front of the piece. ***= I love that part. That's enough.

Never Cross Out Someone's Work

When you put lines through other writer's sentences, you are crossing out their ideas, creativity and love. Just stop it. No "X's" even after you have thrown out that red pen. It's just cruel and unhelpful. If you think someone should remove a block of text, tell the writer in the margin "If you moved this to the end, or maybe even took it out completely, the story would be so much clearer."

Worse, Never Replace Someone's Sentences With Your Own

You might be the greatest language goddess of all time but you are not helping the writer if you change a sentence so it sounds like something you would write. It's confusing at best, condescending at worst. The writer needs to figure that out on his own – you can point out the issue, but don't give a specific solution.

Do Not EDIT. DO NOT EDIT. YOU ARE NOT AN EDITOR ON THIS PIECE

This writer will eventually have an editor. If the piece is strong enough and the writer has the will, that editor will be a professional editor and will make the work as clean and powerful as possible. The writer will also have a copy editor. This person will work in the last stage of the work: the clean up stage. It is a waste of your time, and a waste of the writer's time, to insert semi colons and suggest more conjunctions through out. It's not helpful, it's not fun, and it takes time away from the substantive work you could be focusing on.

5

The Culture Of Feedback – Creating And Enforcing The Language And Vibe

Once you have prepared and arrived at the workshop with written feedback it is easy to feel as though your (hard) work is done. You have made all of the comments you wanted to make; you have said all there is to be said. But you are lucky. Unlike classes in big institutions where instructors have no other means of giving feedback to students but by way of the written feedback on written work, you get to look the writer in the eye and tell him what you think. This can be scary, but if you approach the workshop with good will and the main goal in mind, things will be fine.

OK, so you are a devoted workshop participant now. You care. You are prepared. You spent all last week caring and preparing. You are ready to help.

You walk in and plop yourself down, right next to a writer who has nothing good to say about anything. He's arrogant. She's obnoxious. He's too busy to care; she's in it for the connection to the teacher…and on and on.

You could get up and move, because you know that this person is not going to do anything in the way of being supportive or helpful and you are not having it. But you aren't going to get up. Why? Because you CARE.

Hopefully, the teacher has given you some tools and language so that you are all on the same page in the way of workshop behavior and tone. But that's unlikely. Usually, writers come to workshops with very little preparation - save the reading they have to complete and the (often deficit based) model of feedback they have learned from other workshop and classroom scenarios.

But, don't worry when this happens because you are prepared. Before the session begins, if possible, it is your job to help that negative energy become positive. You need to turn it around. You owe it to yourself and the rest of the room to talk to this negative person about what's great in the work you are about to read (there is always something great, this is never a lie). Try to get them to laugh, offer them a cookie. You are a crusader for kindness: you have to commit to redirect tangents, competition and cruelty before you get going. It'll help everyone. And why are we here? To make sure everyone gets help and improves. If these small positivity tactics don't turn the naysayer around, then you have work to do.

You need to help create the right vibe in the room. You might be alone in this or you might have a cadre of like-minded workshop attendees working on your side. Either way, armed with what you know now, it is your job to help the room exist as a culture of feedback that leads to improvement. The teacher is usually a good ally – if you are in a workshop with a facilitator. But not always. Sometimes it's your job to turn even the leader around.

One way to get a room to be on the same page is to start modeling the behavior you would like to see applied to the work as soon as possible. Of course, one way to be sure to *lose* your fellow writers is to tell them how to behave. So what can you do?

Be Authentically Kind

Make a positive comment about the work you are work-shopping immediately. You will not be lying. No one can possibly write a draft so horrible that you cannot find something beautiful inside. You will be prepared with written comments to draw from so you will already have beautiful places marked in the text. A buffet of kindness is right there at your fingertips.

Be Specific

Don't just say "I like your imagery," Say "I like your imagery in the second paragraph on the third page when you talk about your father's camping trips." Read a sentence aloud that proves your point.

Smile A Little

What an annoying piece of advice, but if you can look the writer in the eye and smile at him, it goes a long way in making him - and the rest of the room - feel calmer and more supported.

When Offering Suggestions, Offer Thoughts, Not Critiques

One of the most maddening words that people use in workshop situations is "critique." There is no reason to criticize work. It devalues the writer's effort, it makes some of the writers feel small where others feel big; it's just cruel. Again, this is not a demand for "nice" for the sake of it. There is a difference between "nice" and "kind." Do not offer platitudes; tell the truth. But do it in a way that does not stand in the way of progress. If we want writers to keep writing we need to give them feedback that has been proven to support improvement. When you have an idea about how something might change be sure to frame it in a way that suggests it's just one idea – not THE idea. Something like: "I wonder if taking the longer description of the fair out of the Prologue might make the reader jump into the action more quickly. I found myself eager for the plot twists that happen in Chapter One."

Introduce Language And Themes You'd Like The Room To Use

Just add one idea at a time - two if you must. Use the language or theme in a piece of feedback. "Could you could do more of what you do on the third page? The imagery is so strong it speaks for itself. I think it could serve the story really well on page four and five as well."

Have Fun

It's sort of amazing to get to leave your work alone for an hour and dive deeply into another writer's work. You get to go inside her mind, into his heart, hang out right there in her gut. When else do you ever get to see the inner workings of a person's psyche with out the filters of daily life or self-consciousness?

So treat it as such. Treat getting involved with other writer's work as a celebration. If you can't stomach the celebration idea – at least look at it like a puzzle. It is your job to make the writer improve and it is your job to make the writer feel like she should care back. Otherwise, skip the workshop and have a brownie.

6

You Are Not A Therapist - You Are Not In Therapy

Something that happens fairly often in writing workshops is that writers cry. Men, women, experienced writers, newbies; it doesn't matter. It's one part stage fright – these are people who rarely see the light of day remember (just like you). But it's something else too. The important work they have toiled over is about to become clay. People may pound the work so that all that's left is a mealy pulp. People may suggest things that feel offensive to the writer. People might hate it.

So people cry. That's fine. Hopefully as people adopt the idea that a workshop should actually be a positive and supportive experience that can happen less. But they still might cry. This stuff is deep. It doesn't have to be a story about abuse or a poem about birds taking flight to be deep. It can be a humorous tale of fantasy witches and the writer still might cry. Because they really, really care about it.

It is important in situations like this that the workshop participants can separate the content from the writing. If it's about funny witches, it's probably not much of a problem, but what if it *is* about abuse? Or fertility? Or love or loss? Often the only way a writer will be able to get to the heart of what he's trying to say is to write *through* the pain. Some times that's the advice that is the most important to give. But we must end there. We must not suggest that the writer leave her boyfriend or go to church or make a public apology or try this doctor or listen to this pod cast. Sure, those are important pieces of information if they are about the written work, but if they are only in service of the content, it's not our place or our expertise. You are not a therapist. A workshop is not therapy. And though it can feel similar – people baring their soul to try to find answers to life's biggest questions – it is not the same. It's dangerous to believe that you can treat a fellow writer in a therapy-like way. That's why therapists take years to become therapists; that's why writers often need them. Just not in a workshop.

This Is Not About You

You might have all of the best ideas in the history of good ideas. You may have figured out how to get the writer out of the weeds. *Just tweak this part here. You are so wonderful at dialogue – how about more. What if the whole piece started right here in the end?* More often than not the writer is going to look at you, furrow her brow, and disagree. Remember, this piece is her baby. She has spent months and years on this and you have spent two hours and a pot of coffee. She knows this piece. She knows herself. You still might be right, and thank goodness she will have all of your written feedback to remind her of these ideas when she gets back to her writing cave, but she still might not take your advice.

That's OK.

The workshop is about the writer improving her work. That could look all kinds of ways. She might reject every piece of advice but one, and that one might be the linchpin for the piece. She might take other participant's suggestions over yours and that's OK too – it is a chorus of voices that she has to pick through and choose what she is ready to hear. Don't get upset if all of the work you put into the draft feels for naught. It might be. But every piece of feedback you give informs your own work and your own ability to give good complete feedback in the future. It all helps. Where and how are questions for later.

This Is, Of Course, About You Too

The writer might not have heard the amazing piece of advice that another workshop participant offered, but *you* did. Something that writer over there said about someone else's draft might completely change the way you think about your own piece, or your own process. Make sure you aren't daydreaming or doodling (or texting, please put your phone away) when other people are giving their thoughts. Really listen. There aren't that many problems – in writing or life – that are so particular. Write good ideas down. Apply them to that novel you keep putting aside. Use the feedback where it works for you.

As a recipient of feedback, you have a job to do too. You need to engage in the conversation or the conversation will happen to you and without you. If you are in a workshop in which the writer is not allowed to speak please get up and leave. Sure, the writer shouldn't talk *much*, there is usually only an hour or so of time that the workshop participants can give feedback and if they are taken up with the writer's stream of consciousness the writer won't get what he needs. Nevertheless, the writer should feel like he has a voice at the table. It's absurd for the group to talk about the work as if the writer isn't in the room. It is ridiculous to talk about something that is factually just wrong when the writer could clear it up in one minute, and it's condescending to talk about someone in the third person when she is sitting right next to you.

This isn't a popular stance, by the way. Many MFA programs and writers' workshops are predicated on the model in which the writer must only sit and listen. So maybe you can't get up and leave. Maybe you have to make this workshop work because you need to graduate. Maybe you need to sit and take it. Please remember that in not being able to speak you are entering into an environment that will necessarily be unbalanced and try hard not to let it get to you. Try as much as you can to remember that your peers are talking about your *work* and not *you*, and that everything they are discussing should be in the service of its improvement.

If you can though, try to attend workshops where everyone has a voice. Participants should ask questions of the writer "Did you mean to leave the prepositions out in this section?" and the writer should be able to ask questions of the group, "I'm really wondering if this character sounds like a teenager or if I have some work to do." Again, specific questions beget specific answers. Please ask them.

How Can I Help, How Can I Help, How Can I Help?

Try to look at the workshop in two parts. You will get help, and then you will give help. Not always in that order. You have little control over the first part. Hopefully, over time with the same people in the same workshop or writing group you can establish a culture and expectation of stellar feedback. But that can take a while. So instead, you can ask for what you need, you can set the tone, you can introduce language and then you need to sit back and listen – both as the writer in the spotlight, and as the peer giving feedback. If you don't listen, you can't help.

As the one giving feedback you should ask again and again "How can I help?" The writer might not be able to tell you exactly what she needs because she really might not know what she needs. But as the workshop participant you are in a position to hear what she might not hear, and see what she might not see. Offer phrases or questions she says back to her, "I think I hear you saying that you aren't feeling happy with the chronology of the piece though you like the flashback sequence, is that what you mean?" Getting a writer to hear what she herself has said to the group is sometimes more helpful than expressing your own thought.

As the writer whose piece is being work-shopped, you also have to listen. That's maybe a bit more obvious, but here's something less obvious: as the writer in the spotlight, you can help too. As we have discussed, you can help guide the workshop with specific questions, you can clear up little moments of confusion in real time, you can mull over suggestions and ask follow up questions to be sure you understand. You can trust that those in the room are there because they care about your work and about you. It's not easy to do. It might take time, but your job in this workshop is to improve, and that isn't going to happen if you don't trust the messengers. Feedback is a two way street.

There are some relatively easy ways to be sure you are a willing participant in the workshop, ready to receive feedback.

Assume Best Intentions

If you have established a helpful workshop and feedback culture, it should be clear that everyone there is there to help you. Remember that. When you are feeling defensive and indignant (which you will feel) try very hard to stop yourself and re-center. No one here is trying to make you feel bad. No one is here to be cruel or competitive. No one is questioning your intent or your devotion.

Often, when we feel defensive it acts as a block between the feedback and us. There are great reasons we have developed this kind of reaction to people telling us that our work is not good enough. Our whole writing lives – hell, our whole lives – people have been telling us our work is not good enough. We have been telling *ourselves* the same thing. And of course it has not been good enough (though *enough for what*? is a good question to ask), this why we come to a workshop. But if we put up that block we are doing a disservice only to ourselves. We can't hear the feedback because there's something in the way.

Filter Your Own Sh-t

Feel inadequate? Feel dumb and without talent? Feel lost? Feel too steeped in the content to spend time concentrating on the language? Join the club. Well, actually you already have; it's called the workshop. Get all of your insecurities and baggage and try really hard to put it all in the corner. You don't need it here. Because if you use all of that sh-t to stand in the way of the feedback you are not going to hear what you need to hear.

Hear The Thing You Least Want To Hear

There is going to be some incredibly annoying (but wise) member of the workshop who is going to confirm your greatest fear about the work. Hear it. Try hard. This person might be the most important person of the day because he knows you well enough to call you on the very thing you were hoping no one would notice. Thank him. And hear what he has to say.

Ask Specific Questions

The workshop should always end with the writer. It's her show. When time is almost finished, someone should take it upon themselves (if they don't the writer must step up) to ask the writer if she has any other questions or thoughts before you wrap up. The writer should have a good five minutes available to ask clarifying questions, or to connect more deeply to a piece of feedback in real time. Everyone else can sit and listen. They have been talking enough.

The writer, in turn, needs to use that time wisely. Go back to the beginning. Ask specific questions and you will get specific answers. If you didn't understand something, ask the person to clarify. If you feel confused about something specific, ask for it to be cleared up. If it's going to take another hour to dig into it, maybe take some time with the feedback and check in about it with the reader later on. Take her out to coffee tomorrow. Check in next week. Do not let the workshop happen to you. You are happening to the workshop.

This Isn't Over: Ongoing Support

Find Your Charlotte

"It is not often that someone comes along who is a true friend and a good writer."
— *E.B. White, Charlotte's Web*

Wilbur, that wise pig, knew one of the most precious truths of revision. He is right; it isn't often that we find someone who is both a good friend and a good writer, but we need to. We all must find our Charlotte. That person who reads with a keen eye and open heart – the person who supports you, knows your writing, and makes brilliant, honest comments that drastically improve your work. And here's the important thing: not all Charlottes are the same for all writers. The reader who works for you might not work for any other writer. What a gift that is, because that means *your* Charlotte will probably be available.

There are some who would say that a reader need not be a friend. Maybe you'll get more brutally honest feedback from someone who doesn't actually like you that much. If she doesn't like you, could she like your writing? Maybe. But if she doesn't like you, could she help you? Maybe not.

Make sure the person who you ask to read is someone who cares about you. Does she have to be your best bar hopping buddy? Your favorite foodie? Does he need to be your BFF? No, and maybe he shouldn't be. This shouldn't be a person who agrees with your every decision. She need not be nice. He should always be kind. She should point out your patterns and show you where you shine. He should suggest structural changes and places you used too many words. She should question the content; she should push for the truth. He should be someone who loves this nearly impossible craft as much as you do, who loves to read and reads books as voraciously as you. She should be enamored of language and she should worry deeply about content. She should care.

We Write In Community

The workshop will work best if the same people come back again and again. The group will strengthen because of the trust that has been built. The friendships will support the work and the work will support the friendships. But we all know that getting a group of artists to commit to a scheduled workshop is unlikely, and besides, now that you have a handle on how to create a workshop culture of feedback for improvement, it won't matter all that much.

If you are lucky enough to have a group that gathers again and again, recognize how fortunate you are. These other writers are your people. They form your community. And while only a few (maybe only one) of them will become your Charlottes, as a group, and individually, they can all help you shape your tangled piece into glory.

Use them. Take their suggestions and roll them around in your mouth, see what they feel like. Say them out loud, see what they sound like. Choose that which you feel truly speaks to the piece and its improvement. And then let the rest go.

The Writer Has The Last Word

As the writer being work-shopped, you will, no doubt, be offered a cacophony of advice, all with the best of intentions. The advice will be contradictory and confusing. Your job as the writer is to take all of the advice as an offering of course, but it doesn't end there. Your main job is to remember that you know the piece and your intention for the piece better than anyone at the table – even your Charlotte. You know what rings true and what you should leave by the wayside. You know that even with the best of intentions, even when your community cares, they will not always be right.

If you are not defensive, if you consider advice seriously, if you care back, in the end it is *you* who has something to say and who gets to decide how to say it. Own that. Remember that there is nothing on that page without you. It is your work and it is your toil and it is your meditation and it is your joy. Everything these people have to say lies on top of all of that. You can thank them, consider their advice, climb back into the cave, and keep going exactly as you have been. It might not be the best idea, but it might be the best idea right now. Whatever keeps you going. You are the writer. You get the last word.

The Last Word

The point of this book is to take you from anxious workshop participant to super confident feedback guru – a person who can turn a negative culture around, be an ever present, insightful support, and a trusted guide. The goal for yourself as the writer is to leave the workshop with clues as to how you might best improve your work, both from the expert advice you have received and from the patterns that you recognize in other writers' work. The goal for the workshop is to want to work together again, create a group that has members who can help each other in an ongoing way. Even if the workshop moves the dial towards improvement just a little bit, it has accomplished what it set out to do. And it will only get better. Trust in it. Bring a hot cup of coffee, a nice blue pen, a kind heart and a sharp eye. The group will be a chorus of useful feedback, a group rivaling even the best in workshop composition, support and guidance. You are all getting better at this, one session at a time. And really, what more could we need?

Works Consulted

Anson, Chris M. *Response Styles and Ways of Knowing, Writing and Response, Theory, Practice and Research.* Ed.   Chris Anson. Urbana: NCTE, 1989.

Sommers, Nancy. *Responding to Student Writers.* Bedford, St. Martin's. Boston/New York, 2013.

White, E.M.*"Post-Structural Literary Criticism and the Response to Student Writing."* College Composition and Communication, 1984.

Yankee, Kathleen Blake. *Reflection in the Writing Classroom.* Logan. Utah State University Press, 1998